ACCESSIBILITY & PUBLISHING

Charleston Briefings: Trending Topics for Information Professionals is a thought-provoking series of brief books concerning innovation in the sphere of libraries, publishing, and technology in scholarly communication. The briefings, growing out of the vital conversations characteristic of the Charleston Conference and *Against the Grain*, will offer valuable insights into the trends shaping our professional lives and the institutions in which we work.

The *Charleston Briefings* are written by authorities who provide an effective, readable overview of their topics—not an academic monograph. The intended audience is busy nonspecialist readers who want to be informed concerning important issues in our industry in an accessible and timely manner.

Matthew Ismail, Editor in Chief

ACCESSIBILITY & PUBLISHING

STEPHANIE S. ROSEN

Copyright © 2018 by Stephanie Rosen
Some rights reserved

This work is licensed under the Creative Commons Attribution-NonCommercial-NoDerivatives 4.0 International License. To view a copy of this license, visit http://creativecommons.org/licenses/by-nc-nd/4.0/ or send a letter to Creative Commons, PO Box 1866, Mountain View, California, 94042, USA.

Published in the United States of America by
ATG LLC (Media)

DOI: http://dx.doi.org/10.3998/mpub.10212548

ISBN 978-1-941269-21-3 (paper)
ISBN 978-1-941269-22-0 (e-book)

against-the-grain.com

This book is dedicated to all the women reading aloud so someone can experience a book, starting with Patricia Bodary Rosen.

CONTENTS

ACKNOWLEDGMENTS

Thank you to my editor Matthew Ismail and to everyone on the publishing team for seeing this project through.

Thank you to my colleagues at the University of Michigan Press for the opportunity to work with a publishing organization that is committed to accessibility. Special thanks to Jon McGlone, LeAnn Fields, and Charles Watkinson for being so wonderful to work with.

Thank you to Anne Cong-Huyen and Steve Pokornowski, for moving to Michigan while I wrote this book.

Thank you to my supervisors at the University of Michigan Library, Meghan Sitar and Laurie Alexander, for completely supporting this project and for genuinely nurturing my success while giving me the freedom to define it.

Thank you to Alex Blaszczuk, for the intense discussions around global disability, and to the Brooklyn Institute for Social Research for fostering our connection.

Thank you to my copyright colleagues at the University of Michigan and especially to Jack Bernard for his feedback on this project.

Thank you to Kei Kaimana for supporting me and to Julian for supporting Kei while I wrote this book.

PART 1

PUBLISHING & ACCESSIBILITY

CHAPTER 1
INTRODUCTION

Accessibility is about equitable access.

Often, *accessibility* refers in particular to equitable access for people with disabilities, a group that comprises about one-fifth of all people alive today and is bound by a common social experience—living in a world of unequal design.

Publishing is about preparing and issuing books, journals, and other materials. In the world of scholarly communication, publishing is especially concerned with quality and impact—quality of content and impact of research.

Accessibility and publishing, the nexus of this briefing, addresses precisely those scholarly concerns of quality and impact. While the movement for accessible publishing is a call for equal access and social justice, it is equally a push for content of the greatest quality and for research with the broadest impact.

In the United States, accessibility is often bound up with discourses of legal compliance. The Americans with Disabilities Act (1990) and other legislations prohibit discrimination against people with disabilities and require that certain things be made "readily accessible to people with disabilities." Compliance is an important foundation for accessibility, but the movement for accessible publishing is much bigger. The aim of accessible publishing is access for all, while the aim of compliance is accommodation for some.

For people with disabilities that affect reading (especially visual, motor, and mobility impairments) accommodations have long been provided by large-scale projects to convert print into specialized formats—tactile type and recorded sound. Today, almost a century after those projects flourished, the digital media ecosystem has changed what accessibility looks like. Now that print publishing workflows are themselves digital and standards for electronic publications have converged around the EPUB format (a free and open e-book file format with the extension .epub), publishers can release books that are "born accessible." A single electronic publication that follows best practices for accessibility can be read across a range of devices and software that adapt content presentation for an individual reader's needs.

This industry shift from an aftermarket of specialized formats to born-accessible publications, from accommodation to universal design, stands to benefit a much broader public. Specialized formats are produced and distributed on a very limited basis and in some cases are only available to those who can prove eligibility according to strict legal definitions of disability. Born-accessible publications can introduce new levels of equity, access, and choice into publishing for new readerships. Scholarship can reach more audiences and be put to new uses. Individual differences in ability and technology can be uncoupled from differences in access. Accessible publishing can drive better design for more readers in more reading environments.

The movement to make publications accessible *when they are published* is a movement to ensure participation by people with print disabilities and a movement to ensure access to information for all. It is a movement to ensure that publicly funded scholarship is available to all members of the public. It is also a movement for quality bookmaking and future-proof formats, to make books now that will work tomorrow on reading systems we have not yet invented. As the practices of publishing shift along with new practices of digital scholarly communication, accessibility has the potential to become the norm.

CHAPTER 2
READING WITH DISABILITIES

As book historian Robert Darnton (1989) noted in an article on the history of reading, "for most people throughout most of history, books had audiences rather than readers" (p. 93). That is, most people in the West between the fifteenth-century invention of the printing press and the nineteenth-century push for universal literacy accessed print by listening to someone else read. In this mediated print landscape, people with disabilities were not necessarily at a disadvantage in accessing the written word. Rather, it was the rise in literacy that also gave rise to print disability: a new condition of being denied unmediated, independent access to print.

Today we think of print disabilities—or print-related disabilities, or disabilities that affect reading, as they are also called—as impairments or differences that affect an individual's ability to see, manipulate, or process print materials. Examples include vision impairments and blindness, differences in dexterity or the upper limbs, and dyslexia or learning disabilities.

"Print disability" is an interesting term, as it emphasizes the role of print in constituting disability. This phrasing reflects the *social model of disability*, a theoretical framework advanced by UK and U.S. disability activists since the 1980s (Shakespeare, 2006). The social model recognizes that individuals have differences and impairments, but it locates disability in the designed environment and ableist attitudes that exclude individuals with impairments. From this framework, for example, it is not blindness that is disabling but print that is, and a differently mediated landscape might be less disabling or differently so.

People with disabilities that affect reading may include, in the United States, the approximately 8 million people who are blind or have difficulty seeing print with corrective lenses, the 36 percent of people over sixty-five who experience severe disability (Brault, 2012), and the rising number of post-secondary students with disabilities (National Center for Education Statistics, 2015). Around the world, people with disabilities that affect reading include the approximately 200 million people with moderate to severe visual impairments (World Health Organization [WHO] & World Bank, 2011).

In the past century, people with visual impairments have gained access to print through processes of conversion. Sighted readers have dictated text aloud, print has been converted into braille, and books have been recorded onto tape. While these processes have provided direct access to print for visually impaired readers, they also represent diminished independence, flexibility, or choice for those readers. Human readers are available limited hours, a small percentage of print works are converted into braille,[1] and recorded audio books have a fixed speed and limited navigation.

Today, digital publications and modern assistive technology can provide these same readers direct, independent, and flexible access to mainstream format publications. Assistive technology is "any technology or device that enhances the capacities of its user (often a user with disabilities)." In the context of reading, *assistive technology* usually refers to screen readers, refreshable braille displays, text-to-speech software, voice command input, and other adaptive input (Rosen, 2017a).

A well-made, accessible digital publication can be used—read, navigated, searched—with equal facility by a tech-savvy user with or without disabilities. The shift to digital media as a dominant format can obviate the need for remediation for readers with disabilities.

Of course, disability is broader than print disability. People with impairments in other sensory capacities such as hearing, with chronic conditions or mental illness, and with other physical differences may all be part of disability communities. And, in a changing publishing landscape of multimedia and digital media, more forms of disability may be said to "affect reading."

1. An estimated 1–7 percent of books are converted into accessible format worldwide (World Intellectual Property Organization, 2016), leading to what many call a "global book famine" for readers with print disabilities.

Fortunately, this increasing complexity is balanced by the converging simplicity of electronic publishing formats. Today, a born-accessible digital publication can be used by and converted for a broad range of individual needs and preferences with readily available software. Accessibility standards, built on research and testing with a broad range of people with disabilities, account for these varying needs to the extent possible and provide guidelines for publications that can be equitably used by a diversity of readers. As digital publishing becomes more prominent, and if accessibility standards are incorporated, the developing media landscape has the potential to become one in which people with disabilities, once again, are not necessarily at a disadvantage in accessing the written word.

CHAPTER 3
UNDERSTANDING ACCESSIBILITY

When we speak of accessibility, several definitions and discourses emerge. The multivalence of the term can be useful, and it can also be confusing. Digital accessibility is not exactly the same as legal accessibility, which is not exactly the same as accessibility in everyday conversation. A brief overview of the definitions and discourses in play will help lay the groundwork for further discussion.

DIGITAL ACCESSIBILITY

Digital accessibility usually refers to a set of technical, testable standards that come from the field of Web accessibility and are codified in the Web Content Accessibility Guidelines (WCAG) (W3C, 2008, 2018) and related documentation. These standards are both a set of basic principles, broadly applicable to many contexts, and a list of specific rules that are more narrowly applicable to modern digital media and technology. The document moves from general to specific, defining digital accessibility and outlining how it is achieved. For example, one of the four basic principles is "Perceivable: Information and user interface components must be presentable to users in ways they can perceive." One corresponding rule (of more than seventy-five total rules) is "All non-text content that is presented to the user has a text alternative that serves the equivalent purpose." Each rule is followed by additional explanation, documentation, examples, and techniques. (This particular rule is best known for requiring that images include "alt text," though it may be satisfied by various techniques.)

These standards date back to the early Internet and were published in their first version in 1999, drawing from and unifying several independent Web accessibility guidelines that developed in the late 1990s (W3C, 1999). The Guidelines, now in Version 2.1 as of 2018, are managed by an international, independent body of experts, the World Wide Web Consortium (W3C). They have been adopted as an international standard (International Organization for Standardization, 2012) and are used as, or form the basis of, legally required Web accessibility standards in several countries.

These standards have also served as the foundation for other related standards and documentation, including the EPUB accessibility standards. EPUB, the open international standard for electronic books, is managed by the International Digital Publishing Forum (IDPF), which as of 2017 is also under the larger organization of the W3C. The combination of these two organizations, IDPF and W3C, means that the standard for electronic publishing is now aligned with Web standards—and their values of longevity, interoperability, and accessibility. Accessible EPUB, which has its own set of testable standards (International Digital Publishing Forum, 2017), is an example of digital accessibility in action.

LEGAL ACCESSIBILITY

Legal accessibility requirements are based around a concept of equitable access for people with disabilities. Equitable access is a flexible framework that may be applied to almost any situation to judge whether a person with disabilities is afforded an equitable experience compared to a person without disabilities. In practice, it relies on both accessibility standards (WCAG and others) and accommodations for people with disabilities (individualized solutions when standards are not implemented or not applicable). In this way, a framework of equitable access provides for both proactive and reactive measures to ensure accessibility.

The guiding accessibility legislation in the United States is the landmark Americans with Disabilities Act (ADA) (1990). The ADA draws from a civil rights tradition and is ultimately concerned with the equal rights, freedoms, and opportunities of people with disabilities in personal, political, and economic life. Like other civil rights legislation, the ADA responds to and prohibits discrimination in the form of "outright intentional exclusion." Unlike other civil rights legislation, it also targets the "discriminatory effects of architectural, transportation, and communication barriers" and uses design standards as a proactive means to counter discrimination by design (§ 12101, 1990). In some cases, then, legal accessibility requirements are exactly the same as digital accessibility requirements, since the law uses those standards to define and enforce accessibility. However, in many cases legal accessibility requires "reasonable accommodations" for an individual who has come up against the barriers of "discriminatory" design (Americans with Disabilities Act of 1990).

Accommodations are used as a regular practice of accessibility in many contexts where the ADA applies. In institutions of higher education, for example, when students need access to published materials that are required for learning but inaccessible, the institution must provide an accommodation—often in the form of an accessible electronic version of the published material. Occasionally, institutions fail to make accommodations, and individuals facing discrimination may pursue legal action. Some such lawsuits have made headlines, but most lead quietly to settlements in which the institution agrees to change its procedures in order to ensure accessibility and enable equitable access to its programs and services. For example, in a 2013 settlement between the University of California Berkeley and Disability Rights Advocates which touched on many areas including access to published materials, the university agreed to "provide students with print disabilities . . . a method by which they may obtain an OCR-scanned digital copy of hard copy printed materials . . . [that are] made available by the Library to non-disabled students."

It is important to emphasize that the ADA applies only to some entities. This settlement and the lawsuit it resolved did not include the publishers who produced hard copy printed materials. The U.S. Department of Justice and the Department of Education's Office of Civil Rights (OCR) (responsible for enforcing the ADA) have not pursued a publisher for the "discriminatory" design of print. This scenario could however come to pass: some U.S. states and Canadian provinces already have laws that require educational publishers to deposit accessible electronic versions of their publications to a central registry or supply them on demand (Office of Civil Rights, 1998; "Accessibility Rules for Publishers," 2017). Furthermore, the ADA has been interpreted to apply to some online services with similarities to publishers and platforms. Of particular interest is the interpretation in cases against Netflix and Scribd, online-only services in the business of providing access to digital content. Both cases ruled that the businesses were places of public accommodation (i.e., subject to Title III of the ADA) and must make their platforms and content accessible in order to allow equal participation by consumers with disabilities.

ACCESSIBILITY

Beyond the more narrow definitions of digital and legal accessibility, there is a range of broader meanings attached to accessibility: from ease of use and availability, to economic affordability and rhetorical understandability. While these meanings may appear to span more widely than the specific concerns of readers with print disabilities, they remain connected to the core matter of equitable access, and they certainly affect equitable access for people with disabilities, whose concerns intersect with issues of usability, availability, affordability, and understandability.

Universal design is one approach that explicitly bridges the design needs of people with disabilities and of other groups who tend to be marginalized rather than centered in design considerations (e.g., children and elders, people less familiar with the dominant language, people of atypical size, height, or strength). Digital accessibility standards are influenced by universal design in that both aim to eliminate the need for accommodations by considering and designing for a broad range of needs, abilities, and capacities up front. Universal design as a philosophy also begins to make room for the needs of people who may not claim disability (Linton, 1998) but who nonetheless experience disabilities, or debilities, the effects of which are similar to disability (Puar, 2017).

In reality, the majority of people who stand to benefit from accessibility in publishing may be "outside the reach" of legal accessibility for multiple reasons (Meekosha & Soldatic, 2011, p. 1383). For one, global disability statistics—which estimate one billion people are currently living with disabilities—are based on a metric of functional impairment (WHO & World Bank, 2011). This means that although disability "poses several challenges for measurement," the measured numbers are inflated in one sense: they represent not only those who identify as disabled but also those who experience impairment (WHO & World Bank, 2011, p. 21). Those who experience impairment but do not identify as disabled may include, for example, the 3.8 million Americans over age sixty-five who have difficulty seeing (Brault, 2012, p. 8). Yet, in many contexts self-identification as a person with a disability is a prerequisite for access to the benefits of legal accessibility, in the form of specialized formats or individual accommodations. For another, global disability statistics show that the majority of people with disabilities are currently living in the Global South—80 percent of people with disabilities (Grech & Soldatic, 2016) and 90 percent of people with blindness and low vision (World Intellectual Property Organization, 2016). In these regions, in spite of the broad ratification of the United Nations Convention on the Rights of Persons with Disabilities (United Nations, n.d.) guaranteeing access to communications, education, and technology (Articles 9, 24, and 21), "the promise on paper for greater accessibility has been incongruent with people's public experiences" (Pal et al., 2016, para. 1).

Worldwide, the one billion people with disabilities alive right now have few things in common, but one of them is that the majority may see little benefit from accessibility when it operates as an accommodation for the most savvy and well-connected users. However, accessibility as a widely adopted norm of publishing in the digital age and a value that pushes publishing toward greater access for all would certainly benefit this population and many others.

CHAPTER 4
PUBLISHING FOR ALL

Accessibility is in line with professional values of good bookmaking, equitable access to information, and scholarship for the public good.

PROFESSIONAL VALUES

Publications that meet accessibility standards are necessary for readers with print disabilities but are also simply better for most readers and more useful for machines, systems, and search technologies that interact with publications. Digital accessibility requires accurate, high-quality metadata at all levels of a publication, which make the publication and the digital objects within it more discoverable, sustainable, and searchable. Visual media and multimedia must be translated to text, making their content available to search algorithms and results, and more usable in more reading contexts. The rising popularity of audiobooks (originally developed as a specialized format for accessibility) and the development of artificially intelligent voice "assistants" indicate that listening is becoming a more mainstream mode of interacting with computers and digital content. Everything that makes a publication accessible makes it more ready to be read aloud without the loss of information or functionality. Accessibility is good bookmaking in a changing environment of reading practices and technologies.

Accessibility is an extension of the commitment to equitable access to information, a core value of librarianship. The American Library Association frames this core value as "all information resources . . . regardless of technology, format, or methods of delivery, should be readily, equally, and equitably accessible to all library users" (2004). Publications that meet digital accessibility standards help libraries fulfill this aim of their mission by obviating the need for assistance and conversion at the point of access. When information is not in a readily accessible format, it often means that some users cannot independently review it and must rely on conversion processes (with delays) to access it. Accessible information and publications not only extend independent access to more users but also open up the possibility of more uses: improving discoverability, enabling computationally driven research (Padilla et al., 2018), and preparing for teaching applications. Especially, when publications are accessible in a broad sense, they support collective access and community access, extending the value of equitable access beyond individual needs and specific "access problems" into the realm of transformative justice (Kumbier & Starkey, 2016).

Public access to publications, knowledge, and data is also a basic value of scholarship, especially scholarship that is supported by public institutions and grants. This value is evident in the 2013 Obama White House Office of Science and Technology Policy memorandum on "Increasing Public Access," which requires that articles and data resulting from federally funded research be made freely available to the public and hosted on accessible platforms. This memorandum is a quite explicit attempt to ensure that publicly funded scholarship benefits the public, but a similar rationale can be found in the open access movement, which argues that "research underwritten by colleges and universities should not be published under a profit model that prevents some colleges and universities from accessing the same research" (Rosen, 2017b). Accessibility, broadly construed, can ensure that publicly supported scholarship is available to all members, not just some members, of the public.

LEGAL OBLIGATIONS

In addition to professional values, there are some obligations related to accessibility. A range of legal requirements address accessibility and may be relevant to publishing in different contexts. These regulations do not apply directly to publishers as such, but they apply to the ecosystem around publishing including public and private educational institutions, libraries, and online businesses.

While publishers are not subject to the ADA, the ADA intersects with publishing in the classroom and the library. Educational institutions are required to make their programs and therefore their course materials accessible; libraries have the provisions to make otherwise inaccessible publications accessible for individual patrons; and some specialized libraries have the right, through an exception in copyright law, to make accessible copies of a broad range of published materials.

Furthermore, the ADA has been interpreted to apply to online services—both those with a corresponding physical site and those that are fully online—including some that have similarities to publishers and publishing platforms. Of particular interest are cases against Netflix and Scribd, both fully online and both business that provide access to online digital content. Although both Netflix and Scribd filed motions to dismiss the complaints against them, on the grounds that the ADA applies only to businesses with a physical place, in both cases district judges denied these motions. Both cases led to settlements—between Netflix and the National Association of the Deaf, between Scribd and the National Federation of the Blind—outlining steps toward making the platforms and their content accessible in order to allow equal participation by consumers with disabilities (Disability Rights Education and Defense Fund, 2012; Disability Rights Advocates, 2015).

In some states and provinces, additional legislation applies directly to publishers. "For several years states such as Texas have required publishers of elementary and secondary textbooks to deposit the electronic version of their textbooks into a central registry, where the state then translates the text into braille for elementary and secondary students who are blind. In July 1997, the first state law applicable to publishers of college textbooks was passed [in Arizona]" (OCR, 1998, p. 6). In Ontario, the Accessibility for Ontarians with Disabilities Act (2005) and associated regulations require that publishers of educational or training materials make those materials "accessible or easy to convert into other [accessible] formats" upon request now and as a default by 2025 ("Accessibility Rules for Publishers," 2017).

These examples trace a trend toward legal accessibility requirements in more publishing contexts. But there are limits to what legislation can achieve.

Legislation requires compliance, and compliance is always a minimum. Best practices and innovative solutions are far above compliance. Furthermore, legislation, regulations, and enforcement apparatuses are subject to change and thus subject to changing political power. In 2015, the United States celebrated the twenty-fifth anniversary of the ADA, a landmark legislation that applied civil rights frameworks to populations with disabilities and has achieved great progress in reducing discrimination and barriers. However, in 2017, U.S. congressperson Ted Poe introduced H.R.620, the "ADA Education and Reform Act," which partially dismantles the current working parts of ADA enforcement, giving businesses that are out of compliance with the ADA design guidelines an almost indefinite period in which they face no real consequences. In 2018, the U.S. Department of Education's Office of Civil Rights, responsible for enforcing the ADA as it applies to educational institutions, made changes to its case-processing manual that narrows what qualifies as a complaint and expands the grounds for dismissal without investigation (Osgood, 2018).

Legislation has real limits, and compliance with legal obligations is merely the minimum. The professional values of publishing, librarianship, and scholarship—values of good bookmaking, access to information, and impact of research—demand that we do better than what is required. The range of strategies and case studies in the next section demonstrates the diversity of activities that go into accessibility and to meeting obligations in various contexts. They span from the retroactive practices of conversion for accessibility to the forward-looking practices of incorporating accessibility into new publications and publishing platforms.

PART 2

STRATEGIES & CASE STUDIES

CHAPTER 5
CONVERSION

Since print is not accessible to a range of people with disabilities that affect reading, making texts accessible has long meant remediating print by reading it aloud or converting it into other stable media that may be used independently by print-disabled readers. Reading to the blind was a staple charitable activity, often performed by upper-class women, around the turn of the twentieth century, and human readers have remained an important accommodation, especially in educational contexts, well into the present age. Meanwhile, large-scale investment in the conversion of publications into accessible formats (especially braille and audio recordings) has built up a significant collection of special format publications and a library system to distribute them to readers with qualifying disabilities in the United States. Today, the National Library Service for the Blind and Physically Handicapped continues to operate—making its constantly growing collection of accessible publications available to readers with print disabilities—alongside newer, digital databases of accessible texts and publisher-driven initiatives for born-accessible content. Even as the publishing industry shifts to digital-first and born-accessible publications, conversion remains a necessary accommodation and common practice to adapt existing publications to meet the needs of readers who cannot access them in their current format.

NATIONAL LIBRARY SERVICE

In the United States, the large-scale program for converting print books into formats for readers with print disabilities is the National Library Service for the Blind and Physically Handicapped (NLS). This service was established in 1931 through the Pratt-Smoot Act, which authorized the Librarian of Congress to select an annual list of titles to be converted, appropriated funds for conversion into braille by specialized printers such as the American Printing House for the Blind, and designated regional libraries as distribution centers for special format works for blind readers (NLS, n.d.). Throughout its long history, this service has been marked by expansion and innovation. First designated for "blind adults," the service was expanded to include children in 1952 and "individuals with other physical disabilities that prevent reading regular print" in 1966 (NLS, n.d.). Today it serves more than 800,000 users[1] across 100 regional libraries and outreach centers in all 50 states with a catalog of more than 269,000 books (NLS, n.d.).

While it began as a braille book program, research and development on "talking books" was already under way at the outset of the NLS. The service expanded to include the production and distribution of talking books, recorded audio of a human reader on vinyl records, starting in 1934, and experimented with a variety of record sizes and speeds through the 1960s. By 1969, the service adopted cassette tapes for its recordings and, by 2000, adopted the newly developed DAISY (Digital Accessible Information SYstem) standard for digital talking books (NLS, n.d.). With each change in formats, the NLS was not merely an early adopter but a major driver and developer of emerging technology—in terms of both the recording media and their specialized playback machines. Today, the NLS collects and distributes publications in braille and audio formats on various media: physical materials in embossed braille, audiobooks or magazines on digital cartridges for use with the talking book player, and digital braille or audio files available for download from the NLS Web-based services (NLS, n.d.).

1. The *Report of the National Library Service for the Blind and Physically Handicapped* (NLS, 2012) records "more than 800,000 reader accounts (reader accounts include institutional accounts and multiple service records for patrons using multiple services)."

The NLS remains a key service for U.S. readers with print disabilities, and similar organizations providing specialized library services for print-disabled readers exist in a number of countries, though at differing scales, across the Americas, Europe, Asia, the Middle East, and Africa.[2] However, because "[b]ooks are selected for the NLS collection on the basis of their appeal across a wide range of interests," the collection may not readily support individual research or upper-level education (NLS, n.d.). The collection is 65 percent fiction and 35 percent nonfiction and must meet a high demand for best-sellers, biographies, fiction, and how-to books, as well as the demand for youth books and for all works in Spanish and other languages (NLS, n.d.). Individuals with print disabilities who are reading for research, education, or work may have to look elsewhere for their materials.

COLLEGES AND UNIVERSITIES

Conversion of text into accessible formats still takes place on an as-needed basis in contexts where accessibility is legally mandated and especially where individuals need to read for their education or employment. One such context is higher education. Colleges and universities do a significant amount of work converting publications and education materials into accessible formats.

Most U.S. colleges and universities have a dedicated office to support the accessibility needs of students with disabilities. Postsecondary disability service offices provide a range of services—for example, alternate testing facilities, American Sign Language interpreters—and most "have set up in-house shops to create or attain alternative media" in accessible formats (Dallas & Upton, 2011, p. 39). Colleges and universities have a legal obligation to effectively provide students with learning materials in accessible formats. According to the Department of Education's Office of Civil Rights, the effective provision of accessible formats has three basic components: "timeliness of delivery, accuracy of the translation, and provision in a manner and medium appropriate to the significance of the message and the abilities of the individual with the disability" (OCR, 1998, p.1). The disability services office often acts as a liaison between the student and instructor, communicating with the instructor about

2. The organizations surveyed in the Global Library Survey Final Report (2009) serve as a representative sample, see Section 7: Organizational Responses.

the need for accessible document formats and converting course documents (including "textbooks, PowerPoints, assignments, online readings, scanned readings, handouts" [Bromley, 2017, p. 3]) whenever the instructor is unable to select or produce them in already accessible formats.

Disability service offices use an adaptable workflow of physical scanning, optical character recognition, manual cleanup and, where needed, image description, to deliver the students an accessible format that best meets their needs and technical proficiencies (Bromley, 2017). "Common equipment for this process include high speed and flatbed scanners, a guillotine for cutting book bindings, optical character recognition (OCR) software, and braille embossers. Plastic comb binding machines can be used for rebinding books. Multiple computers and trained staff will be needed to handle large requests for alternative media" (Dallas & Upton, 2011, p. 40).

These offices are not libraries, and they generally do not build collections, preserve materials, or provide cost-free access. Rather, they convert individual materials that instructors have provided or students have acquired, and students usually must provide proof-of-purchase of textbooks before an accessible copy can be given to them from the office (Wolfe & Lee, 2007). Academic libraries may supplement these offices with their own services, converting items from the collection into accessible formats (Spina & Cohen, 2018). All academic libraries may, "with strong confidence . . . provide access to digitized texts for the print-disabled" under the latest interpretations of copyright law (Adler, 2015). However, the extent to which they actually support, publicize, and perform this work varies. Eighty-seven percent of libraries recently surveyed by the Association of Research Libraries reported that they provide staff assistance in copying/scanning/printing library materials for users with disabilities (Spina & Cohen, 2018). Only a few libraries specifically mentioned converting, creating, or obtaining alternate format materials for users with disabilities among the additional services they provide (Spina & Cohen, 2018).

The conversion and creation of accessible-format learning materials, whether performed by libraries or disability service offices, are crucial to the equal participation of students with disabilities, and the work of disability service offices in particular is a keystone of equitable access to postsecondary education. However the work of these offices also represents some of the least optimized and most duplicated work among strategies for accessible publishing. The conversion that takes place within an individual office may repeat conversion work that has already been done elsewhere and, for materials published from around year 2000 and later, may essentially recreate an accessible digital file that already existed at some earlier point in the digital publication workflow. Disability service offices may be aware of this frustrating reality but are nonetheless tasked with meeting the immediate need of the students they serve. Where publishers, media organizations, and individuals have failed to create accessible content, these offices must step in to fill the gap.

There is a growing demand for born-accessible materials within the higher education context, especially as materials become increasingly digital and the benefits of accessible content become more apparent. Born-accessible materials would provide timely and equitable access for students identified with print disabilities; students who experience disability but have not registered with the campus disability service office or disclosed their need for accommodations to their current instructors (usually prerequisites to receiving accessible copies); and students without diagnosed disabilities who may benefit from accessible reading technologies like text-to-speech, increased navigability, and flexibility.

In the meantime—between a future in which all learning materials are accessible and the present in which most are converted locally on demand—there is a growing collection of digital databases of accessible content to supplement local conversion. Some of these databases, begun only a few decades ago, have already built collections of accessible content as large as and larger than the NLS itself.

CHAPTER 6
DIGITAL DATABASES

While the NLS relied on reading aloud and translation into braille, initiatives around the turn of the twenty-first century began to use digitization technology to convert print into e-text or digital content, a new kind of accessible format. Although these projects were not primarily concerned with the needs of readers with disabilities, they relied on technology originally developed in accessibility (optical character recognition) and now are positioned to benefit readers with print disabilities more than any other conversion project. Today, there are various databases that specialize in accessible electronic formats, supplied directly by the publisher or converted from print. To protect copyright and the market value of published content, these databases have strict user permissions and are not available to everyone—not even to everyone with print disabilities. Yet for individuals with print disabilities who are affiliated with U.S. institutions of higher education, millions and millions of accessible publications are now immediately available through databases like HathiTrust, Bookshare, and others, without the need for local conversion.

EARLY DIGITIZATION EFFORTS

Optical character recognition (OCR), used in today's technologies of scanning and document digitization, has its own history in accessibility technology (Mills, 2015). One of the first machines capable of "reading" the light patterns of printed characters and converting them into usable data was developed between 1910 and 1915 expressly as an aid for the blind. The Optophone, developed by the British physicist Fournier d'Albe, was a handheld optical scanner that emitted a distinct audio tone for each printed character it moved over, so that "after learning the character equivalent for the various tones, visually impaired persons were able to 'read' and interpret the printed material" (Schantz, 1982, p. 3). Developments in OCR (multifont OCR and the coupling of OCR with computer-synthesized speech) were likewise driven by accessibility applications for blind users. In the 1960s, OCR emerged as part of research and development for the Kurzweil Reading Machine, a "computer for blind and print-impaired individuals [that] converts printed materials directly into synthesized speech" and allows users to read "with privacy and independence" (Hoff, 2008).

By 1978, the first commercial OCR scanner was marketed broadly and quickly adopted by business, government, and especially "organizations that were paper-laden and had fairly predictable workflows" (Centivany, 2016, p. 26). From the 1980s to the 1990s, major scanning projects for preservation and digital document delivery began at the National Library of Medicine, the National Archives, Cornell University, and University of Michigan (Centivany, 2016, p. 26–28). These early digitization projects, focused on accessibility broadly speaking but not on accessibility for people with disabilities, created among the first scholarly digital repositories of converted electronic texts. They laid the groundwork for later digitization but were quickly surpassed by the turn-of-the-century Google project to scan the world's books.

The period from 1980 onward was also the period in which OCR technologies expanded to include non-Roman alphabets. Given its initial development on writing systems in which each character is bordered by white space, OCR was unprepared to process scripts like Devanagari (the script for Hindi as well as Sanskrit, Marathi, and Nepali) and Arabic (the script for the Arabic language as well as Urdu, Farsi, Chawi, Kardi) (Yadav, Sánchez-Cuadrado & Morato, 2013; Alkhateeba, Doush & Albsoul, 2017). Today, many languages are scannable with readily available OCR systems, although accuracy rates vary by writing system and OCR software, and additional work is necessary to improve accuracy rates and develop methods sensitive to multilingual and multiscript cultures (Yadav, Sánchez-Cuadrado & Morato, 2013; Risam, 2015; Alkhateeba, Doush & Albsoul, 2017).

HATHITRUST

HathiTrust is an online repository of over sixteen million digitized volumes from the holdings of major research libraries, managed under a shared governance structure representing the partner institutions. Its early history began in the Google "mass digitization project," an initiative to scan all the world's books. Following on the heels of several localized, some failed, and some burgeoning large-scale book-scanning projects, Google's project was the first *mass* digitization project that rapidly changed the landscape (Centivany, 2016). Begun in 2002, the project at its height scanned approximately 30,000 volumes per week, which is more than the previous projects, by the "most aggressive and technologically advanced library digitizers," had scanned in a decade (Centivany, 2017, p. 2361).

Although the Google book-scanning project was not pursued on the grounds of accessibility for users with print disabilities, it was quickly put to that use through the agreement between Google and the University of Michigan, which stipulated that the University would retain digital copies of Google-scanned library holdings and could make use of them for Web-based access. Since the University of Michigan library was already engaged in local scanning of holdings when necessary to meet the needs of print-disabled users, this new digital collection provided the opportunity to greatly improve services for those users (Centivany, 2017). As this early effort evolved into the multi-institution project that became HathiTrust, launched in 2008, the provision of access to electronic copies for users with disabilities grew with it. And, as HathiTrust came under legal challenge from groups representing copyright holders for scanned works, so too did this practice, which was eventually argued before the Southern District Court of New York and Second Circuit Court of Appeals, which ruled that HathiTrust's provision of access to print-disabled users did not infringe copyright. HathiTrust and the legal challenges around it have tested and clarified the rights and responsibilities of libraries and universities in meeting the needs of students with print disabilities. (See chapter 11 "Copyright" for more details.)

Today HathiTrust operates with different access levels for the public at large and for affiliates of supporting libraries. Anyone can search the database and read works that are in the public domain, while affiliates at supporting institutions can read in-copyright works owned by their institution. Readers with print disabilities at supporting institutions may additionally read in-copyright works from the complete database by first verifying their eligibility, then requesting works through a designated staff proxy (usually based in the library or a disability service office) (HathiTrust, n.d.). This database represents a giant leap in the volume and breadth of works available in an accessible format for readers with print disabilities, especially in the area of scholarly publications. And for individuals at the more than 120 partner institutions, it represents a huge advance in access to those works. However, this service is not at present available to the reading-disabled public at large.

BOOKSHARE

Bookshare is a repository of over 600,000 accessible digital publications donated directly by publishers or uploaded by individuals. The service originally began as an online collection of works scanned individually by blind readers for their personal use following the maturation of OCR and synthesized text-to-speech technologies (Candela, 2009). On this early model, Bookshare staff would "proofread the contributions to eliminate scanning errors and make them available via the Internet for download to other users" and would also directly "scan books to increase the library collection" (Candela, 2009, p. 124). In the past decade, as publishing workflows became capable of readily producing accessible electronic copies, this original model shifted to one of primarily collecting electronic files directly from publishers. The service also collects scans made by college student disability service offices, taking advantage of and leveraging the conversion work that is done locally in many of these offices but otherwise not usually shared or coordinated across campuses.

Since Bookshare began as a service for blind adult users in particular, it has a focus on accessible and audio formats and is optimized for individual users as well as libraries. Schools and students in the United States have free access to Bookshare (through an award from the U.S. Department of Education Office of Special Education Programs). Non-student individuals in the United States and in any country may get personal access to the database by paying a fee, the cost of which is determined by the World Bank income rating of the country: $50 per year for high-income countries, $20 for upper-middle, and $10 for low. Organizations that serve individuals with print disabilities in any country may likewise pay an income-adjusted fee based on their number of downloads (Bookshare, n.d.).

OTHER MODELS

A slightly different model is found in AccessText, a secure portal through which disability service providers may request, and publishers may supply, accessible versions of books. The service has a focus on educational publications, and membership is limited to "post-secondary educational institutions throughout Canada, the United States and its territories" (AccessText, 2017). Although AccessText is not a repository, many files are available for immediate download because publishers have authorized access to their entire digital catalog, allowing for automatic processing of requests. In the K-12 education context, other options are available. Learning Ally, for example, is a repository of 80,000 audio format "K-12 books including popular fiction, classic literature, textbooks, test prep and study aids" for students with visual impairments or dyslexia (Learning Ally, 2018).

Apart from databases focused on accessible content for readers with print disabilities, most libraries provide access to electronic books and other content through various databases managed by outside entities or vendors. These digital databases have the potential to support accessibility but have been found inaccessible according to digital accessibility standards and effectively unusable by individuals with print disabilities who rely on assistive technology. (See chapter 8 "Platforms.") However, libraries are increasingly demanding accessible electronic resource databases that can be equitably used by all patrons. At present, when these databases fall short, academic libraries may have to locally convert or externally obtain accessible alternate format copies of an item they already licensed as an electronic file. In these and other situations, databases like HathiTrust and Bookshare are key stopgap measures. They work to create, collect, and lawfully circulate accessible digital copies of publications without compromising the value of those publications in the digital marketplace.

CHAPTER 7
BORN ACCESSIBLE

As long as there has been born-digital content, there has been the potential for born-accessible content. Indeed, some early online publications took immediate advantage of this potential and have been creating accessible content for almost two decades. Now, as a greater share of published content becomes digital, and even print publications come from digital, there is greater potential for born-accessible publications.

ACCESSIBILITY IN DIGITAL SCHOLARSHIP ON THE WEB

The language of the Web, HTML, has had accessibility standards published by the World Wide Web Consortium (W3C) since 1999.[1] Some digital scholarship published on the Web has taken these standards into account, thereby leading the way in accessible scholarly publishing.

One of the first examples of this can be found in *Currents: An E-Journal*, the scholarly publication of the Digital Writing and Research Lab (formerly the Computer Writing and Research Lab) at the University of Texas at Austin. This online scholarly journal included editorial guidelines regarding accessible markup in their Submission Guidelines as early as their first issue in 1999[2] and official policy that "all published contributions must meet the

1. WCAG 1.0 was ratified by the W3C in 1999, building largely on the Unified Web Site Accessibility Guidelines (Vanderheiden & Chisholm, 1998), developed by the Trace Research & Development Center at University of Wisconsin, Madison, from 1995 to 1998.
2. The Submission Guidelines (1999) state, "We ask, however, that such submissions take into account reader-access issues, and that they routinely incorporate such accommodations as the inclusion of <alt> tags in any image and the use of content tags (e.g., citation <cite> and emphasis <em> tags) instead of the corresponding physical markup tags (e.g., italics <i> and bold <b> tags) whenever possible."

W3C accessibility standards" as early as 2002 ("Editorial Information," 2002). *Currents* was edited by an early leader in the field of Web accessibility, John Slatin, who was also at the intersections of scholarship and pedagogy. Slatin was an early member of the W3C, a leader in Web accessibility, and the author of a 2001 *Computers and Composition* journal article, "The Art of Alt," which alerted others in the field to the importance of "alt text" for images and other accessibility features in Web design.

Another early example of born-accessible scholarly publishing can be found in *Kairos: A Journal of Rhetoric, Technology, and Pedagogy*. The longest continuously published online peer-reviewed journal in its field, *Kairos* began publication in 1996 and has required accessible submission from its authors since around 2001 (C. Ball, personal communication, March 9, 2018). Later examples include the *Canadian Journal of Disability Studies*, published online, open access, and in accordance with accessibility standards since 2012, and *Disability Studies Quarterly*, online and in accordance with accessibility standards as of 2007.

In each case, the journal has made a commitment to accessibility and achieved it by focusing efforts in two areas. First, by making its own online interface accessible according to WCAG standards and, second, by using submission guidelines and the editorial process to ensure that each submission has met the standards as well. Now that the standards and practices developed for Web accessibility have been repurposed for the electronic book format EPUB, more publishers have the opportunity to take on this role, promoting accessibility through the editorial process for more types of publications, including the key academic genre of the scholarly monograph.

BORN-ACCESSIBLE ELECTRONIC BOOKS

The EPUB electronic publishing standard, from Version 3 forward, combines standards developed for the Web with standards for accessible format books. As Bill Kasdorf (2013) wrote,

> The Working Group released EPUB 3.0 at the Frankfurt Book Fair in October 2011 . . . The new standard is based on HTML5, the lingua franca of the modern Web, along with its companion Web standards CSS3 (cascading style

> sheets, for presentation) and JavaScript (for scripting behaviour-based features like user interaction). Not only does this enable EPUB 3 to accommodate audio, video, interactivity and other important features, it does so in the same way those things are accomplished using modern browsers and other Web technologies. Likewise, it accommodates non-Latin alphabets and both right-to-left and vertical writing; and thanks to the invaluable participation of key staff of the DAISY Consortium on the EPUB 3 Working Group, it was built to be accessible.

EPUB 3 was built to be accessible at multiple levels, with "accessible content at the core, wrapped in semantic structure, and topped off with accessible metadata" (Rothberg, 2018, p. 45). Not only can EPUBs implement accessibility features, but those features "can be exposed in metadata using Schema.org vocabularies inside the EPUB or on a Web page, or using ONIX metadata in the publisher workflow" to provide users, libraries, distributors, and sellers the information to identify which publications are accessible and in what ways (Rothberg, 2018, p. 45). EPUB accessibility metadata enables transparency and discovery for accessible publications, which is crucial to readers who rely on accessibility features and is a great benefit to users and entities who use accessibility features in various ways, such as a reader who prefers to listen to material read aloud or an entity that searches and indexes.

EPUB's potential for accessibility, inside and out, has made it the "'gold standard' in the publishing industry for the production of accessible digital books" (Accessible Books Consortium [ABC], n.d.). Several organizations are working to encourage publishers to adopt the EPUB standard and commit to producing accessible EPUB content. The Society for Disability Studies released an open letter on "Publishing Accessible Books" (n.d.), encouraging publishers to adopt EPUB 3.0 or later for "built-in accessibility (the best solution)." The ABC encourages all publishers to "use the accessibility features of the EPUB3 standard for the production of digital publications" and "include descriptions of the accessibility features of their products in the information they provide to retailers and others in the book supply chain."

For publishers committed to accessibility, adopting EPUB as an output format will be an important step toward achieving accessibility. However, for publishing organizations with a traditional "print-first" workflow, ensuring the output of accessible EPUB will come with challenges. Although print-first publishing workflows are themselves digital, a digital file in the final preprint stages may have lost structural information from earlier stages and may lack accessibility information—both of which are necessary to output an accessible EPUB.

CHALLENGES FOR PUBLISHERS

In a traditional print-first publishing workflow, a book typically follows a pathway "from a manuscript to a designed PDF ready to be printed" (de Bruijn et al., 2015, p. 26). Along that pathway, the content may pass through several proprietary formats, lose some embedded information, and ultimately get optimized for print layout rather than digital delivery. This workflow presents some challenges for digital output, and creating an accessible EPUB from a print-optimized PDF may more closely resemble print conversion than born-accessible publishing, with all the additional labor that comes with it. Changing a traditional workflow to support born-accessible EPUB will be a labor-intensive process of assessment and systemic change. However, it will ensure that future accessibility work is done at the right point in the workflow, by the right people, to optimize output and eliminate unnecessary processes.

As Bill Kasdorf (2018) has explained,

> if the production workflow is properly designed and executed, much of this [remediation] work goes away. Especially if there is an XML-based workflow, and even better if that workflow is designed to produce EPUB 3 as one of its deliverables, then a lot of straightforward text-based books (novels and straightforward non-fiction, even scholarly monographs) are close to being sufficiently accessible at almost no extra cost. . . . Even for books with images, if the workflow provides a mechanism for authors to supply alt text and extended descriptions (and if they are properly instructed how to do that), work is reduced even further.

As this quote suggests, books with images or visual content present additional challenges. Since accessibility standards require that all "nontext content," (images, multimedia, audio, etc.) must have a "textual equivalent," images require textual descriptions that sufficiently communicate their meaning and purpose to a reader who cannot access the original. And because images are fairly common in academic monographs, publishing books with sufficient description of those images may represent a major change in workflow. Although disability service offices that perform text conversion often create description of visual content, born-accessible publications should ensure that description is created as far as possible upstream in the publishing workflow so it becomes an integrated part of the publication. The Describing Visual Resources Toolkit (Rosen, 2017a) has noted, "In academic publications in the arts and humanities, description must be scholarly as well as accessible, and in line with existing standards: metadata, copyright, and disciplinary conventions. It is therefore best managed by the scholars, academic publishers, and arts organizations who create the publications." Ideally, not only publishers but also authors should include image description in their practice, and indeed this is common practice among many scholars writing in disability studies.

Other content features may introduce additional challenges, especially for publications marketed for postsecondary education. In addition to the text itself (including images, tables, and formulae) content categories to consider for accessibility include enhancements, linked content, and contributed content (Bowes, 2018). Enhancements are enrichments including multimedia elements, interactives, labs, assessments, and quizzes; linked content is Internet-based content that becomes part of the user's experience when linked to from the product; and contributed content is user-generated content that is uploaded or shared within the learning experience (e.g., collaborative class projects, online assignments) (Bowes, 2018). All of these content categories introduce additional accessibility considerations. Yet all of them have the potential to be made accessible with intentional workflows and the use of EPUB and accessibility standards.

In all cases and across content types, the ability to achieve accessibility in the product is closely related to education and support for the content creators. This is true whether the content creators are students uploading an assignment to a shared learning management system, authors submitting manuscripts to a publisher, or publishers contributing books and journals to publishing platforms.

CHAPTER 8
PLATFORMS

While publishing platforms have grown far more complex than the first online journals of the 1990s, today's versions still perform the same basic functions: publishing, hosting, and disseminating. And through these functions, platforms have a similar opportunity to promote accessibility in publishing. Even for complex platforms that host author-uploaded content, coordinate peer-review, or measure reader statistics, the steps toward accessibility are the same. Platforms can make a commitment—then adopt workflows and formats to meet it—and set requirements for content—then provide resources to support authors in meeting them. Several examples in recent years, with major incentives from large funding organizations and the government, show this kind of platform-driven accessibility.

MELLON-FUNDED OPEN ACCESS PUBLISHING PLATFORMS

The Andrew W. Mellon Foundation Program in Scholarly Communications began focusing on long-form digital publication in the humanities, with an eye toward the future of the monograph, around 2013 (Waters, 2016). In recent years, this program has conducted a great deal of research and grant-making around the digital monograph and the features that will define it in changing information environments. Funded projects have taken up specific challenges in this area including open access, economic sustainability, reader metrics, and accessibility. Two projects in particular, Fulcrum and Muse-OPEN, have put accessibility at the center of the platform.

Fulcrum is a project led by the University of Michigan in partnership with the University of Minnesota, Indiana University, Northwestern University, and Pennsylvania State University. The platform is designed to host scholarly materials supplementing a monograph, monographs and journals themselves, and "new forms of multimodal publications" in a way that is flexible, durable, and discoverable ("Fulcrum," n.d.). From the beginning, this project has made accessibility a priority in its platform design, "performing accessibility checks and tests and making numerous adjustments to ensure WCAG 2.0 AA compliance" (Baker-Young, 2017), and in its requirements for submitted materials.

The outcome is that the platform is incorporating accessibility at every stage of design and redesign, resulting in a platform that works toward accessibility constantly, even as it grapples with technically difficult implementations, like a custom-built Web-based EPUB reader. Furthermore, the platform requires authors to provide supplemental materials in the service of accessibility, notably textual equivalents for visual and multimedia. This means educating authors and affecting the industry by preparing more authors who care about and better understand preparing accessible publications.

MuseOPEN kicked off in 2016 as a project to host Open Access monographs in the humanities and social sciences alongside the existing Project MUSE collection of scholarly journals in those fields. This Mellon-funded project has made accessibility a priority for its own design and for its content. In 2017, the project posted fifty-six pages of "comprehensive publisher guidelines . . . for maximizing the accessibility of books for users with a variety of disabilities that negatively affect their ability to use Web-based content . . . [including] visual, auditory, physical, speech, cognitive, and neurological deficits" along with a commitment to "update the guidelines as standards and practices evolve" (Queen, 2017).

The commitment to education is key to a platform-driven approach to accessibility in the current publishing landscape. Authors, editors, and publishers who are new to accessibility will require support and in some cases context-specific educational materials, like the MuseOPEN guidelines. Platforms that invest this work into educating their constituents will benefit from quality content that meets format standards for increased accessibility, flexibility, and future compatibility, and the individuals involved in such projects—authors, editors, designers, and programmers—may bring their newly learned accessible practices to other publications, platforms, and projects.

PUBLIC ACCESS TO FEDERALLY FUNDED RESEARCH

In February 2013, the Obama White House Office of Science and Technology Policy (OSTP) released a memorandum on "Increasing Access to the Results of Federally Funded Scientific Research" in which the OSTP stated its commitment to "ensuring that, to the greatest extent and with the fewest constraints possible . . ., the direct results of federally funded scientific research are made available to and useful for the public" (Holdren, 2013, p. 1). The memo set out concrete directives toward this end, requiring that each federal agency with more than $100 million in annual research expenditures would:

- develop a "Public Access Plan" to support increased public access to both scientific publications and digital scientific data resulting from research funded by the federal government (Holdren, 2013); and
- "ensure that publications and metadata are stored in an archival solution that . . . provides access for persons with disabilities consistent with Section 508 of the Rehabilitation Act of 1973" (Holdren, 2013, p. 4).

As a result of this directive, agencies created public access plans and identified public platforms in which accessible publications and datasets could be deposited. The plans and databases for each affected agency may be reviewed in lists compiled by libraries and information organizations (Columbia University Libraries, 2016; CENDI, n.d.; Association of Research Libraries, n.d.). Identified databases have taken additional steps to improve accessibility in terms of compliance with digital accessibility standards and in terms of broad availability via multiple channels. For example, PubMed Central, the database platform identified by multiple government agencies (including the National Institutes of Health, Food and Drug Administration, and

Department of Veterans Affairs) and managed by the National Center for Biotechnology Information and National Library of Medicine—is "making every effort to ensure that our sites are accessible" (S. Helson, personal communication, February 27, 2018). PubMed also provides support and basic conversion technologies to ensure that deposited articles are accessible to users with disabilities and integrates deposited materials with "large NIH research databases such as Genbank and PubChem" to "accelerate scientific discovery" (National Institutes of Health, 2014).

This government-driven mandate for accessibility promotes digital accessibility and equitable access for people with disabilities (508 compliance), as well as public access and open access. It attempts to ensure that knowledge and data produced by publicly funded research is, in turn, available to the public, and not just to some members of the public. Like the Mellon-funded examples, it uses funding as a lever to make change in accessibility, to drive innovation in digital publishing practices and more fully realize the promise of access and the possibilities of born-digital information. In all of these examples the platform is key, positioned as a gateway in the publishing stream that can drive change in multiple directions.

LICENSED ELECTRONIC RESOURCES

Electronic resources—vendor-supplied digital collections to which libraries subscribe and provide access—are another type of platform with the potential to advance accessibility. They represent a growing share of academic library collections and, by 2020, are projected to account for 80 percent of academic library collection-building expenditures (OCLC, 2015). Although e-resource platforms are not usually the publishers of content, as database collections of digital content they have a similar opportunity to commit to accessibility in their own interfaces and promote accessibility in the content they host and disseminate.

The most common types of licensed e-resources are e-journals, e-books, and full-text (aggregated) databases (Johnson et al., 2012), all of which have the potential to take advantage of digital accessibility standards. Unfortunately, research shows that most electronic resource offerings are inaccessible at the platform level, content level, or both. A 2016 crowd-sourced testing project of forty-four major e-book platforms found that only two platforms received a high score (i.e., the platform and content implement 65% or more of the tested accessibility features) and only thirteen received a high potential score (the platform supports 65% or more of tested accessibility features) ("E-book Audit 2016," 2016). Research on electronic journal platforms has found that 25 of 32 major platforms "rated as marginally accessible or inaccessible" (Tatomir & Durrance, 2010, p. 588). Recent evaluations of several platforms for both e-books and e-journals have found that the majority continue to have significant accessibility barriers (Big Ten Academic Alliance, 2018).

We have yet to see an electronic resource vendor use its position as a platform to significantly advance accessibility, making change among its content publishers and for its users. However, librarians "are becoming noisy" about the lagging progress in this area (McNaught, MacMullen, Smith & Dobson, 2018), and some vendors have made major commitments to accessibility for their platforms (EBSCO, n.d.; ProQuest, n.d.). If e-resource platforms continue to improve in accessibility and more publishers begin to produce born-accessible content, the real accessibility of licensed e-resources can change drastically in the near term.

CHAPTER 9
GUIDEBOOKS

Platforms and publishers committing to accessibility may find that their own organizations require a fair amount of education and support, especially as they may be required to take on the role of educating and supporting those who contribute content to them. Many information professionals, organizations, and consortia have come together to create practical guidebooks for the multiple players in accessibility in publishing. Guides on getting started, organizational change, and understanding obligations are now available for everyone interested in making a commitment to accessibility. The following resources, most of which are themselves highly accessible in every sense, are the best available.

ACCESSIBLE PUBLISHING BEST PRACTICE GUIDELINES FOR PUBLISHERS

(Hilderley, 2011)

These guidelines provide useful background on the meaning of accessible publications in the current landscape and practical, usable advice for publishers at all stages of implementation.

QUICK START GUIDE TO ACCESSIBLE PUBLISHING

(Accessible Publishing Working Group, 2016)

This guide makes the case for the value of accessible publishing and offers guidance on the techniques for creating accessible digital content.

BC OPEN TEXTBOOK ACCESSIBILITY TOOLKIT

(Coolidge, Doner, & Robertson, 2015)

This open access toolkit offers resources to support the creation of open and accessible textbooks.

PEARSON GUIDELINES

(Pearson, 2017)

Industry guidelines with a focus on online learning publications and products, and internal interpretation of standards.

INCLUSIVE LEARNING DESIGN HANDBOOK

(Inclusive Design Research Centre, n.d.)

Handbook designed to assist teachers, content creators, Web developers, and others in creating accessible, adaptable, and personalizable educational resources.

DIAGRAM IMAGE DESCRIPTION GUIDELINES

(DIAGRAM Center & National Center for Accessible Media, 2014)

Guidelines for making images in STEM (science, technology, engineering, and mathematics) educational publications accessible to all, with best practices for writing description, examples of description for different image types, and training materials.

DESCRIBING VISUAL RESOURCES TOOLKIT: DESCRIBING VISUAL RESOURCES FOR ACCESSIBILITY IN ARTS AND HUMANITIES PUBLICATIONS

(Rosen, 2017a)

Toolkit designed to support authors, editors, publishers, and arts organizations in advancing the description of visual resources for accessibility in arts and humanities publications.

ACCESSIBLE PUBLISHING KNOWLEDGE BASE

(DAISY Consortium, 2018)

Provides best practices for creating accessible digital publications. Its primary focus is on EPUB, but it can be used as a reference for any HTML-based format.

ACCESSIBLE EPUB 3

(Garrish, 2012)

Practical guide with tips and examples to understand the EPUB 3 format and how to enrich and enhance content for all readers.

PART 3

ADJACENT FIELDS

CHAPTER 10
READING TECHNOLOGY

A conscientious publisher who follows the guidebooks, adopts the standards, and produces publications with accessibility features might be disappointed to learn that some of those very features (codified as they are in international open standards) are dead on arrival in a good number of reading technologies and devices. This is true not only of accessibility features but also of many advanced EPUB features that are not accessibility specific. For example, inline frames within a page will not render on some readers; alternate text for images is ignored on some reading applications; navigation from the table of contents is impossible with some combinations of assistive technology, reading applications, and devices. EPUB features from the most basic to the most innovative are not consistently "supported," that is, they do not function as expected, or are ignored entirely, on many modern reading devices and technologies.

Still, conscientious publishers can take comfort knowing that their publications are ready while the reading technologies and devices are still catching up. Designing digital content for accessibility has always meant, in part, designing for the future. One of the four principles of the Web Content Accessibility Guidelines (W3C, 2008, 2018) is, "Content must be robust enough that it can be interpreted reliably by a wide variety" of technologies, current and future. In their short history, e-reader devices have strongly resisted accessible design, but the advent of tablets and smartphones has shifted accessible development to reading applications rather than dedicated devices. Accessible publications produced today will work as expected on some current reading technologies, though support is still uneven. These publications should, however, work on future reading technologies and have the potential to work on yet undeveloped technologies that may make greater use of the modularization of digital content (de Bruijn et al., 2015) and the translation of accessible content across sensory modalities.

ELECTRONIC READER DEVICES

For all the promise of making reading accessible, the early development of e-readers was marked by competing, proprietary file formats that fragmented progress and limited technology that ignored principles of universal design. While the manufacturers of e-reader devices have not been held to legal accessibility requirements, the educational institutions that quickly adopted them have been, resulting in national attention to the inaccessibility of such devices.

Amazon Kindle, released in 2007, was the first successful e-reader (a second wave after first-generation options including Rocket eBook, developed in 1998, the Sony Librie [2004], and the Sony Reader [2006] [Hansen, 2016]). In 2009, Barnes & Noble released the Nook, which was an e-reader and more, with Wi-Fi connectivity and built-in app-like features including a dictionary and Web browsing. In 2010, Apple introduced the iPad, which rapidly changed the landscape. After that, most of the previous e-readers became tablets to some extent. The next-generation Kindle was the Kindle Fire, a combination of reader and tablet, and the Nook graduated, after a few versions in rapid succession, to the Nook Tablet in 2011.

In the early years of e-readers, several educational institutions participated in pilots to introduce and study their potential use in classrooms. It was in this educational context, subject to the ADA, that e-readers were publicly exposed for their lack of accessible design. In 2009, a lawsuit was brought by the National Federation of the Blind and the American Council of the Blind against Arizona State University, one of several U.S. universities participating in a pilot program with Kindle. The suit was settled in 2010 by an agreement in which four universities agreed "not to use the Amazon Kindle DX ebook reader or other ereaders until they are rendered accessible for blind students" (Blumenstein, 2010).

The year of this settlement was also the year in which the Federal Communications Commission (FCC) passed new regulations on communications technology in the Twenty-First Century Communications and Video Accessibility Act of 2010. The manufacturers of e-readers petitioned the FCC for a waiver to ignore these accessibility regulations, and more than 500 groups including the American Library Association, Association of Research Libraries, and major disability organizations filed comments in opposition to this petition for waiver (Goldberg, 2013). In spite of broad opposition, the waiver was granted for one year in 2014, extended for one year in 2015, and extended indefinitely in 2016, with plans to review in 2019. E-reader device manufacturers continue without real legal accessibility requirements and without strong incentive to make accessible, universally designed products.

Meanwhile, the Department of Education's Office of Civil Rights and the Department of Justice have made clear that these devices shall not be used for content delivery in academic settings that guarantee equal opportunity for learning. In a joint "Dear Colleague Letter" (2010) on electronic book readers, they have written:

> Requiring use of an emerging technology in a classroom environment when the technology is inaccessible to an entire population of individuals with disabilities—individuals with visual disabilities—is discrimination prohibited by the Americans with Disabilities Act of 1990 (ADA) and Section 504 of the Rehabilitation Act of 1973 (Section 504) unless those individuals are provided accommodations or modifications that permit them to receive all the educational benefits provided by the technology in an equally effective and equally integrated manner.

This strongly worded letter discourages higher education institutions from using technologies that fail to comply with accessibility requirements, asking college and university presidents to "take steps to ensure that your college or university refrains from requiring the use of any electronic book reader, or other similar technology, in a teaching or classroom environment as long as the device remains inaccessible to individuals who are blind or have low vision" (U.S. Department of Justice & U.S. Department of Education's Office for Civil Rights, 2010, p. 2). The letter furthermore discourages the use of technological innovations that fail to innovate in the direction of accessibility and emphasizes the potential for the nexus between education and technology to drive new accessible tech: "It is unacceptable for universities to use emerging technology without insisting that this technology be accessible to all students" (U.S. Department of Justice & U.S. Department of Education's Office for Civil Rights, 2010, p. 2).

READING APPS

In today's technology landscape, any tablet, smartphone, or mobile device can act as an electronic reading device. Reading applications or apps, rather than dedicated devices, have become the locus of development, innovation, and improved accessibility. Devices running on either of today's major mobile operating systems—Apple's iOS or Google's Android—already incorporate built-in assistive technology features including text-to-speech, voice input, and options for alternate display. Reading application developers can promote accessibility by ensuring that their apps are compatible with the built-in accessibility features of these operating systems as well as capable of supporting accessible content features.

Yet the many applications capable of reading EPUB are not equally capable of supporting the accessibility features of EPUB. The EPUB Test Project monitors this variability by collecting data from a crowd-sourced testing protocol. The EPUB Test Suite consists of a set of EPUB files that exemplify various EPUB features (some accessibility-related) and instructions for volunteers to download the sample files, open them on a reading platform and device, and then record which features are successfully supported. The resulting spreadsheets show the still stratified landscape of support for standards across combinations of devices, operating systems, applications, and assistive technologies. The results also give readers who rely on assistive technology and accessibility features the information they need to choose reading technologies that will work best. This information may also be useful for publishers who wish to identify and recommend reading systems that support the EPUB features they are making use of and for technology developers who wish to see how their product measures up against the field. Built-in support for EPUB features that are crucial to some readers can be a competitive edge in this still crowded market.

Users with disabilities may have other considerations in choosing reading technology beyond the support for EPUB standards. For example, the cost and compatibility of a technology, the availability of texts on a platform, or the size and weight of a particular device may be make-or-break considerations for a particular user. Research by Allison Kidd (2014) at the University of Colorado provides comparison across these variables. For some users, the simplified features of a dedicated e-reader may be preferable to a tablet—for example, users with light sensitivity may prefer the paper-style screen of an e-reader to the backlit screen of a tablet. In general, the simple interface, lightweight profile, and backlight-free screen of electronic reading devices are important design features for some, including some with disabilities. But the lack of universal design principles means that these features often come along with no tactile controls or audio capabilities and no alternative input compatibility. In short, the devices come with no capability for alternative forms of input or output beyond the smooth interface of the unlit screen, which a broad variety of readers with disabilities cannot effectively see, touch, or operate. Reading applications, which may be coupled with a variety of input and output technologies, hold much more promise for a broader range of readers.

While reading devices and applications continue to catch up to supporting established standards for accessible publications, standards are still crucial for content creators who want to produce accessible publications with the greatest potential to be usable for all. Web standards have been around for years and, although not all mainstream Web browsers support all elements of the standards, standards are still crucial to ensuring relatively functional and equitable user experience of Websites across Web browsers, operating systems, and devices from desktops to tablets. With the merger of International Digital Publishing Forum and World Wide Web Consortium, the EPUB standards are now managed by the same group that has lobbied for, established, and improved modern Web standards over the past two decades. The current EPUB standards are the best bet for the future in terms of accessible content and in terms of designing reading technologies.

CHAPTER 11

COPYRIGHT

As a type of intellectual property law that protects the rights-holder's control over certain uses of a work—including the right to reproduce, create derivative works, or distribute copies—copyright may seem at odds with accessible publishing efforts. Largely, efforts to make published works accessible have precisely been efforts to reproduce, create derivative works of, and distribute copies of works that are unusable in their original format for readers with print disabilities. And indeed there are instances in which copyright may stand in the way of efforts to make publications more accessible. However, copyright also gives users the right to make certain uses of works without permission, and the terms of copyright are largely favorable to the uses associated with access for readers with print disabilities. There are some exceptions, and there are important steps that all players (authors, publishers, vendors, libraries, users) may take now in order to ensure that copyright law continues to enable uses associated with accessibility.

CHAFFEE AMENDMENT

In U.S. Copyright Law, there are "exceptions" to the protections of copyright in which a user of a work need not ask permission of the owner of a work for certain, defined uses. Two of these exceptions apply to uses associated with accessibility: Section 121, or the Chafee Amendment, and Section 107, or Fair Use.

In the current United States Copyright Code, Section 121 allows nonprofit organizations or governmental agencies to provide alternative accessible copies of previously published nondramatic literary works in specialized formats exclusively for use by blind or other persons with disabilities. This powerful amendment, introduced by Senator John Chafee and signed into law by President Bill Clinton in 1996, accelerated and expanded the specialized production of accessible format works for readers with print disabilities. Prior to this amendment, the special format conversion houses that created copies for the National Library Service (NLS) would not begin a single step of conversion before receiving permission from the rights holder, resulting in a greater lag time between print and accessible versions, a backlog of unprocessed but in-demand works, and a list of "off limits" works for which the owner would not grant permission. It is a wonder that the NLS operated as successfully as it did under these conditions, but following the passage of this amendment, the NLS operated with greater freedom and less friction in its processes to build a catalog of accessible works.

Yet the powerful provision of the Chafee Amendment is closely hewn. As Lingane and Fruchterman (2003) put it, "The essence of the social bargain between publishers and the disability community was to provide easier access to people with disabilities while protecting the economic interests of publishers. Chafee was drawn narrowly to seal this bargain." The amendment is narrow in its definitions of every relevant term. It is narrow in defining the entity who may make alternative accessible copies, the type of work that may be copied, the format in which the copy may be distributed and, of course and always, the audience who may exclusively use the copy—"blind or other persons with disabilities."

Under Chafee, the protections for making alternate accessible copies of works cannot be enjoyed by any entity or individual but only by an "authorized entity." Such an entity must be "a nonprofit organization or a governmental agency" and must have "a primary mission to provide specialized services" to "blind or other persons with disabilities," and those services must be "relating to training, education, or adaptive reading or information access needs" (17 U.S.C. § 121 (d)(1)). Such a definition obviously applies to the conversion houses of the NLS but less obviously to educational institutions, libraries not serving a specialized population, and other organizations that serve the general public.

Furthermore, not just any work can be copied—only "nondramatic literary works." *Nondramatic* leaves out musicals, plays, and motion pictures, while *literary*—defined as works "expressed in words, numbers, or other verbal or numerical symbols or indicia, regardless of the nature of the material objects . . . in which they are embodied"—leaves out visual, performative, and audiovisual works and sound recordings. This means that works that fall outside of the "nondramatic literary" definition are unaffected by the Chafee Amendment and, for the purposes of the NLS, are treated in the same way as they have been since 1931, with a request for permission sent to the rights holder and the hope that permission will be granted, and quickly.

Finally, not just any type of copy can be made. Chafee protects the creation and distribution of copies in "specialized formats," a term that includes "braille, audio, or digital text" or, "with respect to print instructional materials, includes large print formats" (17 USC § 121(d)(4)). And these alternate format copies must be, and can only be, "distributed exclusively for use by blind or other persons with disabilities" (17 USC § 121(d)(4)). This final limiting clause governs the entire thrust and intent of the amendment. The amendment is intended to allow for uses of a work that serves people with print disabilities, and it is also intended to ensure that such uses do not interfere with any uses of the work in other spheres, with the market and distribution of the work in general, or with the entire ecosystem in which the work is lawfully used, copied, bought, and sold.

The line drawn around this protection, and the qualification of an "authorized entity" in particular, has generated controversy between rights holders whose interest is in protecting the distribution and market value of a work, and educational and cultural heritage organizations whose interest is in serving the public, some members of whom are blind or have print disabilities.

Colleges, universities, and libraries have been particular sites of disagreements. The Association of Higher Education and Disability (AHEAD), a professional organization for student disability services offices, holds that "colleges and universities, and especially their disability service offices, should be recognized as 'authorized entities' as defined under the Chafee Amendment"

(AHEAD, 2006, p. 5). Judge Baer, in a landmark decision on *HathiTrust v. Authors Guild*, noted that "the ADA requires that libraries of educational institutions have a primary mission to reproduce and distribute their collections to print-disabled individuals, making each library a potential 'authorized entity'" and concluded that a university "has 'a primary mission' to provide access for print-disabled individuals, and it is consequently an authorized entity under the Chafee Amendment" (Baer, 2012, pp. 22–23).

FAIR USE

The Author's Guild appealed Judge Baer's 2012 decision, and an Appeals Court found that the large-scale digitization of books in HathiTrust and access to the digital copies for users with print disabilities did not infringe on copyright because of Fair Use. The decision reaffirmed that the transformative use of works, that is, digitizing them and making them available for search and research, was a clear example of Fair Use.

For most libraries that make digital accessible copies of works for individual users with print disabilities as such needs arise, it is Fair Use rather than the Chaffee Amendment that protects this activity. Long before mass digitization projects, the House Report on the Copyright Act of 1976 stated that "the making of copies or phonorecords of works in the special forms needed for the use of blind persons" is a "special instance illustrating the application of the fair use doctrine" (ARL, 2012).

The HathiTrust decisions and other recent decisions have given libraries more standing in creating accessible copies for patrons with print disabilities in particular, especially "where there is strong evidence of a public policy favoring access from the courts, from legislative history, and from other laws favoring the activity, and where the market has apparently failed completely to serve a given community, courts can invoke fair use to protect an institution that provides access to otherwise inaccessible works" (Butler, 2015, p. 5). That is, even when digitization is not transformational (e.g., the digitization of a single work for the purposes of reading the work), this use is nonetheless justified "because of the special circumstances of the disabled" (Band, 2015, p. 5). In a future in which accessible versions of new publications are readily available, this argument may no longer hold. However in a present reality in which accessible versions are rarely available, local conversion for the purposes of print-disabled access is justified.

INTERNATIONAL TREATIES

The copyright laws discussed earlier apply to the U.S. context. The United States is also party to international copyright treaties—the Berne Convention and bilateral agreements—that require the United States to respect the copyright of works originating in other countries. However, given the U.S. Copyright Law exceptions, those works can also be converted for the use of people with disabilities under Chafee Amendment and Fair Use. For a user and a library in another country, however, the use (conversion) of a work would depend upon the copyright laws and exceptions in that country. "Over 50 (primarily developed) countries have adopted exceptions that allow the making and distribution of accessible format copies. However, over 130 WIPO countries, in which the majority of print disabled people live, do not have copyright exceptions relating to the print disabled" (Band, 2013a).

The Marrakesh Treaty, developed by the World Intellecutal Property Organization's (WIPO) Standing Committee on Copyright and Related Rights, is meant to address this disparity across countries and to support the sharing, across national borders, of accessible copies for users with print disabilities. The treaty was signed in Marrakesh, Morocco, in 2013, by fifty-one countries (a WIPO record for initial signatories) and entered into force in 2016 when it reached twenty ratifying countries (World Blind Union [WBU], n.d.). Today it has been ratified by thirty-seven countries whose "citizens can now benefit from the increase in accessible materials through cross-border sharing and the increased production of books under the Treaty's provisions" (WBU, n.d.). The ratification especially benefits "those countries that do not have existing limitations and exceptions in their laws to address access by persons who are print disabled or do not have large numbers of accessible-format works" (Cox, 2015, p. 15).

The Marrakesh Treaty also stands to benefit countries like the United States, as Krista Cox (2015) has explained:

> The United States, for example, already has the Chafee Amendment (which permits the creation of accessible-format works), the fair use doctrine, and exceptions to the rules governing import and export. However, if a

> print-disabled person in the United States seeks an accessible-format copy produced in another country, the copyright law in that country might prevent the export of the accessible copy to the United States. The Marrakesh Treaty would solve this problem by permitting authorized entities to import and export accessible format works for beneficiary persons, allowing entities to share resources.
>
> In addition to allowing for the sharing of books between countries with a common language, the Marrakesh Treaty would benefit the print-disabled in the United States who speak other languages. In the US, approximately 13 percent of the population speaks Spanish. The United States also has a significant number of persons who speak Chinese, Tagalog, French, Vietnamese, German, Korean, Russian, Arabic, Italian, and Portuguese. Native speakers of these languages would benefit from the cross-border exchange provisions of the Marrakesh Treaty.

As of 2018, the United States has signed the treaty but not ratified it. "U.S. law currently complies with the Treaty, and the United States could ratify the Treaty without amending the Title 17" (Band, 2013b). Ratification remains important, however, because as Jonathan Band has explained, "the Treaty should result in more Contracting Parties adopting exceptions permitting authorized entities to make accessible format copies and to export them to other Contracting Parties, including the United States. This will be particularly helpful to the print disabled in the United States that are interested in reading foreign language books" (Band, 2013b, p. 21).

CONCLUSION

Accessibility and publishing is currently a diverse set of activities designed to meet the needs of readers with disabilities and to shift toward publishing practices that better support equitable access for all.

The history of accessibility and publishing is not a simple narrative of progress, but a recursive story of progress and resistance. Major changes in technology have brought with them new possibilities for equality, new forms of inequity, and even new paradigms of ability and disability, as the print revolution eventually brought mass literacy and print disability. Manufacturers of e-readers fought against requirements for accessible devices and copyright holders fought against the transformation of their works for readers with print disabilities. The progress made in these fields has been against concerted resistance and only through the persistent campaigns of dedicated individuals, often at the level of the law. The realm of higher education has consistently been a space for pushing the possibilities of accessibility.

Efforts towards accessibility have led in unpredictable directions. The crucial technology of OCR and the popular consumer format of the audiobook are both byproducts of innovation in the service of making publications accessible. We do not know what byproducts our current accessibility efforts will produce, just as we do not know what future reading technologies will eventually parse the accessible publications we make today. Advances in accessibility may come in the form of play and of art and performance practice. Accessibility supports yet unknown technologies and acts of reading.

Accessibility supports disability as we know it and as it will inevitably change. Much of the world's disabled population is underserved or unserved by access predicated on legally recognized disability status. The mechanisms for determining ability status may themselves have discriminatory effects, even when functioning correctly. For example, in the United States a person who has permanently lost her sight may have to repeatedly certify her impairment to retain benefits, filling out a 34 page form from the Social Service Administration every year (Samuels, 2014, p. 123). In other contexts, the scene of requesting accommodations may produce what has been called the masquerade of disability (Siebers, 2008) or "performances of proving" disability—"exaggerating a limp, carrying a cane not strictly needed, or otherwise performing to stereotypical expectations of disabled bodies" (Samuels, 2014, p. 133). And in many contexts, the idea of disability status may be unavailable for populations who are subject to debilitation including the risk and "inevitable injury" of war, unsafe labor conditions, and environmental toxicities (Puar, 2017).

Accessibility, when pursued in the fullest sense, may produce a publishing ecosystem that will better serve readers with print disabilities, readers with yet unrecognized disabilities and debilities, and reading that is differently mediated. Accessibility is for the future. At present, everyone in the information professions has a role to play in accessibility, and actors positioned at the gateways of the publishing process and publishing platforms have the opportunity to drive a great amount of change. Over the next several years, accessibility has the potential to become as mundane as the practices of citation—a given in scholarly communication that is taught and practiced at all levels and quietly undergirds larger practices of knowledge sharing and discovery. Accessibility has the potential to become a norm in scholarly publishing and to make equitable access normal.

REFERENCES

Accessibility Rules for Publishers. (2017, June 26). Retrieved March 19, 2018, from https://www.ontario.ca/page/accessibility-rules-publishers

Accessible Books Consortium. (n.d.). Accessible Publishing. Retrieved May 13, 2018, from http://www.accessiblebooksconsortium.org/publishing/en/

Accessible Publishing Working Group. (2016). *BISG Quick Start Guide to Accessible Publishing*. New York: Book Industry Study Group.

AccessText. (2017). AccessText Network. Retrieved May 7, 2018, from http://www.accesstext.org/index.php/

Adler, P. S. (2015). Special Issue on Copyright. *Research Library Issues: A Report from ARL, CNI, and SPARC* (285), 1–2. Retrieved from https://doi.org/10.29242/rli.285

AHEAD. (2006). Position Statement: AHEAD's Perspective on the Issues of Textbook Access. AIM: The Advisory Commission on Accessible Instructional Materials in Postsecondary Education for Students with Disabilities. Retrieved from https://www2.ed.gov/about/bdscomm/list/aim/meeting/4-1-2001-teleconference/ahead-position-paper.doc

Alkhateeb, F., Abu Doush, I., & Albsoul, A. (2017). Arabic optical character recognition software: A review. *Pattern Recognition and Image Analysis, 27*(4), 763–776. https://doi.org/10.1134/S105466181704006X

American Library Association. (2004, June 29). Core values of librarianship. Retrieved from http://www.ala.org/advocacy/intfreedom/corevalues

Americans with Disabilities Act of 1990, Pub. L. No. 101–336, 328 (1990).

Association of Research Libraries. (2012). Briefing: Accessibility, the Chafee Amendment, and Fair Use. Association of Research Libraries. Retrieved from http://www.arl.org/focus-areas/copyright-ip/fair-use/code-of-best-practices/2445-briefing-accessibility-the-chafee-amendment-and-fair-use#.WqaC8JPwaAw

Association of Research Libraries. (n.d.). Access to Federally Funded Research. Retrieved from http://www.arl.org/focus-areas/public-access-policies/federally-funded-research#.WvhhD9MvyAx

Baer, D. J. H. *The Authors Guild, Inc., et al., against HathiTrust, et al.* (United States District Court, Southern District of New York, October 10, 2012). Retrieved from https://www.eff.org/files/hathitrust_decision_copy_2.pdf

Baker-Young, M. (2017, December 18). Fulcrum Year End Update - 2017 Edition. Retrieved February 19, 2018, from https://www.fulcrum.org/blog/2017/12/18/year-end-update/

Band, J. (2013a, August 6). The Marrakesh Treaty. Retrieved May 14, 2018, from http://policynotes.arl.org/?p=92

Band, J. (2013b, October 10). A User Guide to the Marrakesh Treaty. Library Copyright Alliance. Retrieved from http://www.librarycopyrightalliance.org/storage/documents/user-guide-marrakesh-treaty-1013final.pdf

Band, J. (2015). What Does the HathiTrust Decision Mean for Libraries? *Research Library Issues: A Report from ARL, CNI, and SPARC* (285), 7–13. https://doi.org/10.29242/rli.285

Big Ten Academic Alliance. (2018). Library E-Resource Accessibility - Testing. Retrieved May 13, 2018, from https://www.btaa.org/library/accessibility/library-e-resource-accessibility—testing

Blumenstein, L. (2010). Kindle Accessibility Suit Settled with Universities. *Library Journal*, 18.

Bookshare. (n.d.). Bookshare. Retrieved May 14, 2018, from https://www.bookshare.org/cms/

Bowes, F. (2018). An Overview of Content Accessibility Issues Experienced by Educational Publishers: A Current Overview of Content Accessibility. *Learned Publishing, 31*(1), 35–38. https://doi.org/10.1002/leap.1145

Brault, M. W. (2012). *Americans with Disabilities: 2010*. Washington, DC: U.S. Census Bureau.

Bromley, M. J. (2017, November 2). *Guidelines for Creating Accessible Digital Materials for Blind Students*. Portland State University. Retrieved from https://www.ahead.org/about-ahead/about-overview/special-interest-groups/blind-and-low-vision

Butler, B. (2015). Fair Use Rising: Full-Text Access and Repurposing in Recent Case Law. *Research Library Issues: A Report from ARL, CNI, and SPARC* (285), 3–6. https://doi.org/10.29242/rli.285

Candela, A. C. (2009). Bookshare. In S. Burch (Ed.), *Encyclopedia of American Disability History* (pp. 124–125). New York: Facts on File.

CENDI. (n.d.). Implementation of Public Access Programs in Federal Agencies. Retrieved May 13, 2018, from https://cendi.gov/projects/Public_Access_Plans_US_Fed_Agencies.html

Centivany, A. L. (2016). *Understanding Organizational Responses to Innovative Deviance: A Case Study of HathiTrust* (Dissertation). University of Michigan, Ann Arbor.

Centivany, Alissa. (2017). The Dark History of HathiTrust. In *Proceedings of the 50th Annual Hawaii International Conference on Systems Science.*

Columbia University Libraries. (2016, November 18). Public Access Mandates for federally Funded Research. Retrieved May 13, 2018, from https://scholcomm.columbia.edu/open-access/public-access-mandates-for-federally-funded-research/

Coolidge, A., Doner, S., & Robertson, T. (2015). *B.C. Open Textbook Accessibility Toolkit.* British Columbia: BCcampus. Retrieved from http://opentextbc.ca/accessibilitytoolkit/

Copyright Law of the United States, 17 U.S.C. § 101. Retrieved from https://www.copyright.gov/title17/92chap1.html

Cox, K. (2015). International Copyright Developments: From the Marrakesh Treaty to Trade Agreements. *Research Library Issues: A Report from ARL, CNI, and SPARC* (285), 14–22. https://doi.org/10.29242/rli.285

DAISY Consortium. (2018). Accessible Publishing Knowledge Base. Retrieved May 14, 2018, from http://kb.daisy.org/publishing/

Dallas, B. K., & Upton, T. D. (2011). Maximizing Access to Postsecondary Educational Print Materials for Students with Print-Related Disabilities. *Journal of Applied Rehabilitation Counseling, 42*(1), 35–42.

Darnton, R. (1989). Toward a History of Reading. *The Wilson Quarterly, 13*(4), 86–102.

de Bruijn, M., Castro, L., Kircz, J., Lorusso, S., Murtaugh, M., Rasch, M., . . . Wu, A. (2015). *From Print to Ebooks: A Hybrid Publishing Toolkit for the Arts.* Amsterdam: Institute of network cultures.

DIAGRAM Center, & National Center for Accessible Media. (2014). Image Description Guidelines. Retrieved from http://diagramcenter.org/table-of-contents-2.html

Disability Rights Advocates. (2015, November 19). National Federation of the Blind and Scribd Agree to Collaborate to Make Reading Subscription Service Accessible to the Blind. Retrieved May 14, 2018, from http://dralegal.org/press/national-federation-of-the-blind-and-scribd-agree-to-collaborate-to-make-reading-subscription-service-accessible-to-the-blind/

Disability Rights Advocates. (2013, May 6). Settlement, University of California, Berkeley. Retrieved from http://dralegal.org/wp-content/uploads/2012/09/settlement-ucb_0.pdf

Disability Rights Education and Defense Fund. (2012, October 10). *National Association of the Deaf v. Netflix.* Retrieved May 14, 2018, from https://dredf.org/captioning/

E-book Audit 2016. (2016, November). Retrieved May 14, 2018, from https://sites.google.com/site/ebookaudit2016/home

EBSCO. (n.d.). Accessibility. Retrieved May 14, 2018, from https://www.ebsco.com/technology/accessibility

Editorial Information. (2002). *Currents: An E-Journal,* (6). Retrieved from https://currents.dwrl.utexas.edu/spring02/index.html

Fulcrum. (n.d.). Retrieved February 19, 2018, from https://www.fulcrum.org/

Garrish, M. (2012). *Accessible EPUB 3.* Sebastopol, CA: O'Reilly. Retrieved from http://public.eblib.com/choice/publicfullrecord.aspx?p=860821

Global Library Survey Final Report. (2009). Rightscom Ltd. Retrieved from http://www.daisy.org/projects/global-accessible-library/survey_final_report.html#s1

Goldberg, B. (2013). E-Reader Firms Fight Rules Requiring Accessibility. *American Libraries, 44*(11/12), 16.

Grech, S., & Soldatic, K. (2016). *Disability in the Global South: The Critical Handbook.* Cham, Switzerland: Springer International Publishing.

Hansen, J. (2016). E-Reader. In *The Social Media Revolution: An Economic Encyclopedia of Friending, Following, Texting, and Connecting.* Santa Barbara, CA: Greenwood.

HathiTrust. (n.d.). About. Retrieved May 7, 2018, from https://www.hathitrust.org/about

Hilderley, S. (2011, April). Accessible Publishing Best Practice Guidelines for Publishers. Retrieved from http://www.accessiblebooksconsortium.org/inclusive_publishing/en/accessible_best_practice_guidelines_for_publishers.html

Hoff, H. E. (2008). Kurzweil Reading Machine. In C. R. Reynolds & E. Fletcher-Janzen (Eds.), *Encyclopedia of Special Education.* Hoboken, NJ: John Wiley & Sons, Inc. https://doi.org/10.1002/9780470373699.speced1215

Holdren, J. P. (2013, February 22). *Memorandum on Increasing Access to the Results of Federally Funded Scientific Research.* Office of Science and Technology Policy. Retrieved from https://obamawhitehouse.archives.gov/sites/default/files/microsites/ostp/ostp_public_access_memo_2013.pdf

Inclusive Design Research Centre. (n.d.). Floe Inclusive Learning Design Handbook. Retrieved May 14, 2018, from https://handbook.floeproject.org/

International Digital Publishing Forum. (2017, January 5). EPUB Accessibility 1.0: Conformance and Discovery Requirements for EPUB Publications. Retrieved from http://www.idpf.org/epub/a11y/accessibility.html

International Organization for Standardization. (2012). *Information technology - W3C Web Content Accessibility Guidelines (WCAG) 2.0* (ISO/IEC 40500:2012). Retrieved from https://www.iso.org/standard/58625.html

Johnson, S., Evensen, O. G., Gelfand, J., Lammers, G., & Zilper, N. (2012, January). Key Issues for e-Resource Collection Development: A Guide for Libraries. International Federation of Library Associations and Institutions. Retrieved from https://www.ifla.org/files/assets/acquisition-collection-development/publications/electronic-resource-guide-2012.pdf

Kasdorf, B. (2013). Key Issue - EPUB 3's Coming of Age. *Insights: The UKSG Journal, 26*(2), 210–213. https://doi.org/10.1629/2048-7754.06

Kasdorf, B. (2018). Why Accessibility Is Hard and How to Make It Easier: Lessons from Publishers. *Learned Publishing, 31*(1), 11–18. https://doi.org/10.1002/leap.1146

Kidd, A. (2014, March). How to Choose E-Books & E-Readers for Accessibility – 2014. Retrieved May 14, 2018, from http://atrc.colostate.edu/files/quickstarts/E-Books_E-Readers_Accessibility_3-2014.pdf

Kumbier, A., & Starkey, J. (2016). Access Is Not Problem Solving: Disability Justice and Libraries. *Library Trends, 64*(3), 468–491.

Learning Ally. (2018). Learning Ally. Retrieved May 7, 2018, from http://www.learningally.org/

Lingane, A., & Fruchterman, J. (2003). The Chafee Amendment: Improving Access to Information. *Information Technology and Disabilities, 9*(1). Retrieved from http://link.galegroup.com/apps/doc/A205363897/AONE?u=lom_umichanna&sid=AONE&xid=b3629966

Linton, S. (1998). *Claiming Disability: Knowledge and Identity*. New York: New York University Press.

McNaught, A., MacMullen, R., Smith, S., & Dobson, V. (2018). Evaluating E-book Platforms: Lessons from the E-book Accessibility Audit: Evaluating E-book Platforms. *Learned Publishing, 31*(1), 5–10. https://doi.org/10.1002/leap.1143

Meekosha, H., & Soldatic, K. (2011). Human Rights and the Global South: The Case of Disability. *Third World Quarterly, 32*(8), 1383–1397. https://doi.org/10.1080/01436597.2011.614800

Mills, M. (2015, January 5). Optophones and Musical Print. Retrieved May 14, 2018, from https://soundstudiesblog.com/2015/01/05/optophones-and-musical-print/

National Center for Education Statistics. (2015). *Digest of Education Statistics: 2013*. Retrieved from https://nces.ed.gov/programs/digest/d13/

National Institutes of Health. (2014, March 25). Frequently Asked Questions about the NIH Public Access Policy. Retrieved May 13, 2018, from https://publicaccess.nih.gov/FAQ.htm

National Library Service. (2012). *Report of the National Library Service for the Blind and Physically Handicapped 2012*. Retrieved from https://www.loc.gov/nls/about/organization/reports-speeches/report-national-library-service-blind-physically-handicapped-2012/

National Library Service. (n.d.). The National Library Service for the Blind and Physically Handicapped. Retrieved May 14, 2018, from https://www.loc.gov/nls/about/

OCLC. (2015). *Meeting the E-resources Challenge: An OCLC Report on Effective Management, Access and Delivery of Electronic Collections*.

Office of Civil Rights. (1998, January 9). OCR Docket 09–97–2145 1998.

Osgood, D. (2018, March 5). Taking Stock of the Key Changes to OCR's New Case Processing Manual. Retrieved May 14, 2018, from https://www.hmbr.com/news-insight/taking-stock-of-the-key-changes-to-ocrs-new-case-processing-manual/

Padilla, T., Allen, L., Varner, S., Potvin, S., Roke, E. R., & Frost, H. (2018). Always Already Computational. Retrieved May 14, 2018, from https://collectionsasdata.github.io/

Pal, J., Chandra, P., O'Neill, T., Youngman, M., Jones, J., Song, J. H., . . . Ferrari, L. (2016). An Accessibility Infrastructure for the Global South (pp. 1–11). Proceedings of the 8th International Conference on Information and Communication Technologies and Development. ACM Press. New York, NY. https://doi.org/10.1145/2909609.2909666

Pearson. (2017). Pearson Guidelines. Retrieved from http://wps.pearsoned.com/accessibility/

Poe, T. ADA Education and Reform Act of 2017, Pub. L. No. H.R. 620 (2017). Retrieved from https://www.congress.gov/bill/115th-congress/house-bill/620

ProQuest. (n.d.). ProQuest Accessibility. Retrieved May 14, 2018, from https://www.proquest.com/company/ProQuest-ADA-Compliance.html

Puar, J. K. (2017). *The Right to Maim: Debility, Capacity, Disability*. Durham, NC: Duke University Press.

Queen, W. (2017, June 7). Update on Muse OPEN. Retrieved from https://t.e2ma.net/message/5h8egd/xz0il

Risam, R. (2015, May 31). Across Two (Imperial) Cultures [blog]. Retrieved May 2, 2018, from http://roopikarisam.com/uncategorized/across-two-imperial-cultures-2/

Rosen, S. (2017a). Describing Visual Resources Toolkit. Retrieved May 4, 2018, from https://describingvisualresources.org/

Rosen, S. (2017b, February 3). Making Projects Accessible. [Blog post]. Retrieved May 14, 2018, from https://sites.lsa.umich.edu/collaboratory/category/blog/

Rothberg, M. (2018). Publishing with Accessibility Standards from the Inside Out: Accessibility Standards from the Inside Out. *Learned Publishing, 31*(1), 45–47. https://doi.org/10.1002/leap.1149

Schantz, H. F. (1982). *The History of OCR, Optical Character Recognition*. Manchester Center, VT: Recognition Technologies Users Association.

Shakespeare, T. (2006). *Disability Rights and Wrongs*. New York: Routledge.

Slatin, J. M. (2001). The Art of ALT: Toward a More Accessible Web. *Computers and Composition, 18*(1), 73–81.

Society for Disability Studies. (n.d.). Publishing Accessible Books. Retrieved June 10, 2016, from http://www.disstudies.org/Publishing%20Accessible%20Books

Spina, C., & Cohen, M. (2018). *SPEC Kit 358: Accessibility and Universal Design (May 2018)*. Association of Research Libraries. https://doi.org/10.29242/spec.358

Tatomir, J., & Durrance, J. C. (2010). Overcoming the Information Gap: Measuring the Accessibility of Library Databases to Adaptive Technology Users. *Library Hi Tech, 28*(4), 577–594. https://doi.org/10.1108/07378831011096240

United Nations. (n.d.). Convention on the Rights of Persons with Disabilities (CRPD). Retrieved May 14, 2018, from https://www.un.org/development/desa/disabilities/convention-on-the-rights-of-persons-with-disabilities.html

U.S. Department of Justice, & U.S. Department of Education, Office for Civil Rights. (2010, January 19). Joint "Dear Colleague" Letter: Electronic Book Readers.

Vanderheiden, G. C., & Chisholm, W. A. (1998, January 20). Unified Web Site Accessibility Guidelines, Version 8. Retrieved from https://www.w3.org/WAI/GL/central.htm#REF.Ref

W3C. (1999, May 5). Web Content Accessibility Guidelines 1.0. Retrieved April 24, 2018, from https://www.w3.org/TR/WAinternetCONTENT/

W3C. (2008, December 11). Web Content Accessibility Guidelines 2.0. Retrieved from http://www.w3.org/TR/WCAG20/

W3C. (2018, June 5). Web Content Accessibility Guidelines 2.1. Retrieved from https://www.w3.org/TR/WCAG21/

Waters, D. J. (2016, July 22). Monograph Publishing in the Digital Age. Retrieved February 22, 2018, from https://mellon.org/resources/shared-experiences-blog/monograph-publishing-digital-age/

Wolfe, G. L., & Lee, C. (2007). Promising Practices for Providing Alternative Media to Postsecondary Students with Print Disabilities. *Learning Disabilities Research & Practice*, *22*(4), 256–263. https://doi.org/10.1111/j.1540-5826.2007.00254.x

World Blind Union. (n.d.). Marrakesh Treaty Ratification and Implementation Campaign. Retrieved May 14, 2018, from http://www.worldblindunion.org/English/our-work/our-priorities/Pages/right-2-read-campaign.aspx

World Health Organization, & World Bank. (2011). *World Report on Disability*. Geneva, Switzerland: World Health Organization.

World Intellecutal Property Organization. (2016). The Marrakesh Treaty – Helping to End the Global Book Famine. Retrieved from http://www.wipo.int/edocs/pubdocs/en/wipo_pub_marrakesh_overview.pdf

Yadav, D., Sanchez-Cuadrado, S., & Morato, J. (2013). Optical Character Recognition for Hindi Language Using a Neural-Network Approach. *Journal of Information Processing Systems*, *9*(1), 117–140. https://doi.org/10.3745/JIPS.2013.9.1.117

ABOUT THE AUTHOR

Stephanie S. Rosen is a librarian scholar who brings insights from disability studies—and its intersections with feminist, queer, and critical race studies—into library administration and digital scholarship. She is Associate Librarian and Accessibility Specialist at the University of Michigan Library and holds a PhD in English from University of Texas at Austin.

www.ingramcontent.com/pod-product-compliance
Lightning Source LLC
Chambersburg PA
CBHW051351290326
41933CB00043B/3452

* 9 7 8 1 9 4 1 2 6 9 2 1 3 *